God is My
Helper

God is My Helper

By V. Gilbert Beers
Illustrated by Robert Boehmer

ZONDERVAN
PUBLISHING HOUSE OF THE ZONDERVAN CORPORATION
GRAND RAPIDS, MICHIGAN 49506

Learning to Read from the Bible Series

GOD IS MY HELPER
GOD IS MY FRIEND
JESUS IS MY TEACHER
JESUS IS MY GUIDE

GOD IS MY HELPER
© 1973 by V. GILBERT BEERS

Library of Congress Catalog Card Number 72-85561

Printed in the United States of America

What's in This Book

Wise Men Share Their Best

Matthew 2:1-12

A Boy Shares His Food

Matthew 14:13-21

Mark 6:31-44

Luke 9:10-17

John 6:1-14

Doing What God Wants

Abraham Obeys God

Genesis 22:1-14

Moses Obeys God

Exodus 2:23 — 4:17

Nehemiah Does What God Wants

Nehemiah 1 — 8

Being Sorry

God's People Are Sorry

Jesus Tells How to Be Sorry

The Boy Who Was Sorry

What These Stories Teach

Basic Word List

New Word List

Introduction

God Is My Helper is a brave venture into territory that has not been previously explored. It gives the new reader rephrased Bible stories that are structured so as to reinforce the lessons for living that our children have already heard.

Under any circumstances the simple proclamation of deep truth is a demanding intellectual exercise. When, as here, it must be done with a limited vocabulary for a beginning reader, some measure of the difficulty of the project is apparent.

It is most appropriate that Christian parents and teachers capture the mind of a newly independent reader with material that enriches the understanding of biblical scenes and causes the reader to respond to the implications of its message. Our failure to do this may be measured by the tragic host of children and young people who have a vague idea of the biblical record and no idea of the lessons that the Word intends for their lives.

This book should not be given to the eager new reader and then forgotten. The child should be encouraged to return and "Read to Daddy" so that parent and child can talk about the story and its applications. By helping the child to think as well as to read, the real value of *God Is My Helper* will be realized.

We are convinced that there is a need for more books of this sort for the newly independent reader. We trust that the path blazed by this volume will encourage many others to write for young readers.

The National Association of Christian Schools welcomes this addition to the classroom bookshelf and trusts that the response of Christian parents and teachers will generate a demand for many similar volumes.

John F. Blanchard, Jr.
Former Executive Director,
National Association of Christian Schools

A Word to Parents and Teachers

Now that your child has learned to read, new horizons have opened to him. In his pre-reading years, he depended on you to explain things to him. Much of his learning was filtered through teacher or parent.

But reading has brought your child into the world of discovery. Much that he learns now comes from books which are written at his reading level.

There are many beginning-reader books written for public school use — communicating science, social action, and other important learning to the child.

But there are few books for the beginning reader which help him learn the Bible. This book has been written to help satisfy the need for Bible materials at the child's own reading level.

It is important for the beginning reader to enjoy the great stories of the Bible, but he also should see these stories in the context of lessons to be learned and how those lessons shape his life.

This volume introduces Bible readings to the child in the context of what he will learn from them. For example, stories which teach sharing are grouped under this heading.

After each story, helps are given at the child's own reading level. These guide him in discovering new words, new thoughts, and new applications from the Bible reading.

A basic vocabulary list is given at the back of this volume. All readings are built from this basic list, in addition to the few new words introduced with each reading.

New words are listed with each reading under the heading, "New Words I Have Learned," and a cumulative list of all new words is given at the back of the volume.

This book may be used as a supplementary reading book in Christian day schools or in Sunday schools. Parents will find that it brings new life to family devotions, for the child can take a more active part by reading Bible selections himself. Your child will also find delight in "reading Bible" in his own quiet reading time.

It is my prayer that this book will help your child find a new excitement in discovering the Bible as he reads it "all by himself."

V. Gilbert Beers

God
Takes Care
of Me

God Gives a Beautiful World

Once there was no world at all. There were no boys or girls. There were no mothers or fathers.

The wide sky had nothing in it. It had no stars or moon to give light at night. It had no sun to give light in the day time.

God made a beautiful world
and gave it to you and me.

There were no animals or birds. There were no trees or flowers.

God thought about all these things. "I will make a world," God said. "I will put boys and girls in My world. I will put mothers and fathers

Adam and Eve were very happy, for God gave them all they needed.

there to take care of them. I will give them animals and birds and fish. I will make flowers and trees for them to see."

So God did all that He said He would do. He made a beautiful world. God made lakes and rivers and mountains.

God put birds and animals and fish in His world. He made flowers and grass and trees. He put a sun and moon and stars in His sky.

"I will make a father and a mother first," God said.

God made a father and a mother. He called them Adam and Eve.

"Take care of all that is in My beautiful world," God said.

Adam and Eve looked at God's world. They were very happy.

"God gave us animals and birds and fish

Find some pictures of things God made.

to eat," said Adam. "He gave us many other foods, too. We will never be hungry."

"God also gave us a beautiful home where we can live," said Eve.

God took care of Adam and Eve. He gave them all they needed. God takes care of fathers and mothers and boys and girls now, too.

New Words I Have Learned

Adam	Eve	moon
God	star	sun

New Thoughts to Think About

1. Who made the world? Who made you?

2. Can a man take care of a house that he made? Can God take care of a world that He made? Can God take care of you?

3. Have you ever thanked God for His beautiful world? Have you ever thanked Him for taking care of you? Why not thank Him for these things now?

New Things for Me to Do

Cut out some pictures of things God made. Find pictures of the moon, stars, and the world. Cut out pictures of trees, animals, and birds. What other pictures did you find?

God Takes Care of Joseph

"Look at that coat!" one of Joseph's brothers said. "Father gave it to Joseph."

"Father gives Joseph many things," said another brother. "I do not like Joseph. He gets more than I do."

The brothers talked much about Joseph. They became very angry as they talked. They became angry at Joseph.

**Joseph's brothers became angry
and sold him as a slave.**

God took care of Joseph
and gave him many good things.

"We must kill Joseph," said one brother.
"No," said another brother. "We will sell him. Then he will work as a slave."

So Joseph's brothers sold him. Some men took Joseph to another country to make him work as a slave.

But God took care of Joseph. A kind man took Joseph to live in his house.

One day the man's wife said something bad about Joseph. The man put Joseph in jail.

Joseph was very sad. The jail was not a good place to live. But Joseph talked with God each day.

"God will take care of me," Joseph thought.

God did take care of Joseph. Soon Joseph was put over all the other men in jail.

One day a man came to see Joseph. "The king wants to talk to you," he said.

Joseph hurried to see the king. "What can I do for you?" he asked.

"I want someone to tell me about my dreams," the king said.

God helped Joseph know about the king's dreams. So Joseph told the king what God had said.

"You are a good man," the king said. "I will put you over all of my people."

The king put Joseph over all the people in his country. Joseph was very happy.

"God took care of me," said Joseph. "I will thank Him each day because He is so good to me."

Ask God to help you each day.

New Words I Have Learned

brother	dream	Joseph
jail	slave	wife
	coat	

New Thoughts to Think About

1. What did God do for Joseph when he needed help?

2. Do you think God will help you when you need it? Does He want you to ask Him for help?

3. Do you need help for something now? Ask God to help you. See what He will do.

New Things for Me to Do

Write the word **Ask** on something. Put it in your room where you can see it. Think about this word each day. Then ask God to help you each day.

Food for Hungry People

"I want some water," a little boy said.

"We want some water, too," said his mother and father. "But we have no water."

No one had water. There were no wells or rivers or lakes.

Suddenly someone shouted. "I see water!" he said.

Everyone hurried to drink some water. But they could not drink it. It did not taste good.

Everyone hurried to drink the water.

Now the people were very sad. They had water, but they could not drink it.

"What will we do?" the people asked. Then they began to say bad things about their leader, Moses.

Moses was very sad. He wanted his people to have water to drink. Moses began to talk with God.

God showed Moses a tree. "Put that tree into the water," God told Moses. "Then the water will be good to drink."

Moses and some men cut down the tree. They put it into the water. Then the water was good to drink. Soon the people had all the water they wanted.

One day the people began to say bad things about Moses again. "We do not have enough food to eat. Moses and his God do not give us enough food."

God sent birds for the people to eat.

Moses was sad when he heard the people say these things. "God will give you food to eat," he said.

God did give the people food to eat. Soon many birds came down on the ground. The people caught the birds so they could eat them.

Then God gave little pieces of bread to the people. Every day the bread came on the ground. The people picked it up and ate it. They called this bread manna.

"God gave us food to eat," the people said. "We must never say bad things about God again. God takes care of us. He will not let us be hungry."

Who gave you good food to eat?

New Words I Have Learned

caught   piece   manna
Moses   drink   taste

New Thoughts to Think About

1. Who gave water and food to the people? What kind of food did they have?
2. Would you have any food to eat if God did not give it? God made all the food you eat.
3. The next time you eat, think about your food. Think how God gave it. Did you thank Him for it?

New Things for Me to Do

Make pictures of some food you eat. Or cut out pictures of food you like. Put these pictures together. They will help you think about the food God gives you.

Sharing
What
I Have

The woman and her husband were so glad to have Elisha eat with them.

Some Good People Share Their House

"Is that Elisha?" a woman asked. "Is that the man who does God's work?"

The woman's husband looked at a man walking into town. "Yes," he said. "That is Elisha, the man who does God's work."

"Hurry," said the woman. "Ask Elisha and his helper to eat at our house."

So her husband ran to get Elisha and his helper.

The woman and her husband were so glad to have Elisha eat with them. "Please eat with us every time you come back to our town," the woman said.

Every time Elisha and his helper came back to town, they ate with the good woman and her husband.

"Come with me," the woman said to Elisha one day. "I have something to show you."

Elisha and his helper went with the woman. She took them to a beautiful room.

"My husband and I want you to have this room," she said. "We made it for you and your helper. Every time you come to town, you may stay here."

Elisha smiled when he looked around the room. It was a beautiful place.

Elisha smiled when he saw the
beautiful room.

"You even gave us a table, and a chair, and a lamp," said Elisha. "And you gave us a good bed so we can sleep here."

"My husband and I are glad to help someone who works for God," the woman said.

"Thank you," said Elisha. "I am glad to know people who want to share their house with me."

How can you share what you have with others?

New Words I Have Learned

Elisha   lamp   husband
                                share

New Thoughts to Think About

1. How did the woman and her husband share their house? Why did they do this?
2. Why does God want us to share with others?
3. How can you share what you have? What can you do now?

New Things for Me to Do

Ask Mother or Father to help you write down some of the things you can share with others. Each day share something with someone. You will want to share God's Word. You will also want to share what you know about Jesus.

The wise men looked for a new king.

Wise Men Share Their Best

"Look!" a wise man said one day. "A new star is in the sky. Do you see it?"

"Yes, we see the star," said another wise man. "That is the star we must follow. It will take us to a new king."

The wise men knew that the star would lead
them to a new king. This king had been sent
by God.

The wise men rode on some camels. They
followed the star for many days.

At last the wise men came to a city. "Where can we find the new king?" the wise men asked some people.

"A new king?" the people said. "We have only one king. His name is Herod."

"Another king?" asked Herod, when he heard what the people said. "I am the only king here.

The wise men were very happy when they found Jesus.

I can not have another king in my country. I must find this king and kill him."

King Herod talked with the wise men. "I have heard that the new king is in Bethlehem," he said. "When you find him, tell me who he is."

The wise men went to Bethlehem. The star went, too. It went before them until it stopped over a house.

"He is here!" the wise men said. When they went into the house, they found Jesus, the new king. They were very happy.

"We have brought our best gifts for the new king," the wise men told Mary and Joseph. Then they gave their gifts to Jesus.

That night God told the wise men about King Herod. He told them that Herod wanted to kill Jesus. He told them to go back home some other way.

The next day the wise men left for their home. But they did not go back to King Herod. They did what God had told them. They knew they must obey God.

"No one must kill the new king," they said. "We know that God sent Him. He is God's Son."

The wise men were very happy that they had seen God's Son. They were very happy that they could give Him their best gifts.

How can you give your best to God?

New Words I Have Learned

Bethlehem   camel   Herod

Son   Mary   wise

                      Jesus

New Thoughts to Think About

1. Did the wise men give Jesus their best gifts? What kind of gifts does God give us?

2. What kind of gifts do you give God? Do you give Him your best?

3. What did you give to God last week? What will you give Him this week?

New Things for Me to Do

Think about the gifts you can give to God. Write down some of them or ask Mother or Father to help you. Here are some you can write:

    I can give God some money.

    I can talk to God.

    I can sing to God.

    I can go to God's house.

    I can tell others about God.

A Boy Shares His Food

"Mother! Mother!"
a boy shouted as he ran
into his house. "My friends are
going around the lake to see Jesus.
May I go, too? Please?"

The boy's mother smiled. "Yes,
you may go," she said. "But be
careful."

"I will," said the boy. "May
I have some food to take
along?"

The mother looked
in her kitchen. She
found five little
loaves of bread
and two fish.
She put the food into a
little basket.

**The boy was happy that he could
share his food with Jesus.**

The boy took the basket of food. He ran to be with his friends. They talked and laughed as they walked around the big lake.

"Look at all those people," the boy said to his friends. "We will never get to see Jesus now."

The boy and his friends sat down on the ground. They could hear Jesus. But they were very sad that they could not see Him.

Jesus talked for a long time. He said many wonderful things about God. The boy and his friends listened to all that Jesus said.

At last it was evening. "I'm hungry," said the boy. "I'll share my food with you," he said to his friends.

The boy and his friends took the bread and fish from the basket. But before they could eat the food, they heard someone shouting.

"Does anyone have food?" a man called. "Jesus wants some food."

The boy looked at his friends. "Let's give our food to Jesus," he said.

So the boy and his friends took their food to Jesus. They watched Jesus break many pieces

Everyone had food to eat.

You can share your money with Jesus.
You may help someone far away get a Bible.

from the bread and fish. Soon the mothers and fathers and boys and girls had all they wanted to eat. Jesus could do this because He was God's Son.

Jesus smiled at the boy. He gave the boy and his friends some food to eat, too.

The boy was so glad he had shared his food with Jesus. But he was too happy to say anything. So he sat down near Jesus and ate his bread and fish.

New Words I Have Learned

cent   careful   loaves

evening   listen   Bible

New Thoughts to Think About

1. Why did the boy share his food with Jesus?
What if he had kept it all? Did the boy help
Jesus do His work?

2. Can you help Jesus by sharing what you have
with Him? What can you share with Him?

New Things for Me to Do

Ask some friends to do this with you. Ten of
you each could give one cent each day. In one
year you would have $36.50 to share with Jesus.
Then you could ask someone to buy Bibles for
children who do not have any. This would help
Jesus do His work.

Doing
What
God Wants

Abraham Obeys God

One day God talked to Abraham. "There is something you must do for Me," God said.

"I will do anything for You," said Abraham.

"Then take your son, Isaac, to a mountain," God said. "Burn him on an altar."

Abraham went away
to do what God said.

Abraham was afraid. He was very sad, too.
How could God ask him to do this?

"I told God I would do anything for Him,"

**God sent an animal
to take Isaac's place.**

Abraham thought. "Now I must do what He said."

So Abraham took his son, Isaac, up on a mountain. He made a stone altar. People in those days killed animals and burned them on stone altars. That was one way they told God, "We love You. We will obey You."

"Where is the animal?" Isaac asked. "We must have an animal to burn on the altar."

Then Abraham told Isaac what God had said. He told his son what he must do.

Isaac knew that his father must obey God. So Isaac lay down on the altar. He would do anything God told him to do.

Then an angel called to Abraham. "Don't do anything to your son," the angel said. "God knows now that you will do anything He says. God does not want you to hurt your son."

Abraham was so happy. He knew now that God never did want him to hurt Isaac.

God just wanted to know if Abraham would obey Him. He wanted to know if Abraham would do anything for Him.

The Bible tells us what God wants.

New Words I Have Learned

Abraham	altar	angel
burn	Isaac	stone

New Thoughts to Think About

1. Would Abraham have done anything for God? How do you know?

2. Would you do anything God says?

3. What are some things God wants you to do for Him?

New Things for Me to Do

Will you do one of these now?

Pray.

Learn something from the Bible.

Tell someone about Jesus.

Give some money for God's work.

Ask someone to go to God's house with you.

Moses was very sad. He thought much about his people in Egypt.

"They are all slaves," Moses thought. "They work all day for the bad king. But the king will not let them do what they want."

Moses looked at his sheep. He liked to take care of sheep. He liked to go with his sheep into the fields. He liked to go with them near the mountains.

"My sheep are happy," Moses thought. "They do not have to work for anyone. They can do what they want."

Moses thought about the time when he had

**Moses saw something
he had never seen before.**

lived in Egypt. He had lived with the king and the princess.

Moses had not been a slave. People who lived with the king and princess did not work as slaves.

But one day the king had been very angry with Moses. Moses had to run away from Egypt to hide.

Moses went far away from Egypt to another country. There he took care of sheep.

Suddenly Moses saw a bush on fire. The fire would not stop. But the bush did not burn up.

Moses walked near the bush. He wanted to see it.

Then God talked to Moses. "Do you see the fire that does not stop?" God asked Moses. "I can do many other things like that."

Moses knew then that God was talking to him. Men could not do the wonderful things that God could do.

"I want you to take your people away from Egypt," God told Moses.

"I want you to go back to Egypt," God said.
"I want you to take your people away from
Egypt."

Moses was afraid. He did not want to do this. But he knew that he must obey God.

So Moses did what God said. He went back to Egypt. He took all his people away from the bad king. They did not have to work for the king again.

Do you do what your mother and father want you to do?

New Words I Have Learned

bush   Egypt   princess

New Thoughts to Think About

1. How did Moses obey God?
2. Do you obey God? Do you obey your mother and father? Do you obey them as much as you should?

New Things for Me to Do

What are some things Mother or Father want you to do each day? Think of the things they want you to do most. Do you do them all? Do you do any of them? See how many you can do now. Then see how many you can do each day this week.

The king was glad that he could help Nehemiah.

Nehemiah Does What God Wants

"Why are you so sad?" the king asked Nehemiah one day.

Nehemiah lived in a country far away from his home. He was the king's helper in this country.

"I'm thinking of our beautiful city back home," Nehemiah said. "Long ago some people tore it down. They tore the walls down, too. Those beautiful walls have never been put together again."

"But what do you want me to do?" the king asked.

"Please let me go home to my city," Nehemiah said. "Let me take some men with me. They will help me put the walls together again."

The king smiled. He was glad that he could help this good man.

"I will let you go," the king said. "You may put the walls together again."

Nehemiah took some soldiers with him. He took a letter from the king. The letter said that Nehemiah could put the walls together again.

The men in the city were happy to see Nehemiah. They helped him find people to work on the walls. Soon many people were putting the walls together.

But some people outside the city did not like this. They were afraid.

"Nehemiah must not put the walls together," they said. "If he does, the city will be too strong. Then we can never take it."

These people tried to keep Nehemiah from putting the walls together. But God helped

Some people did not want Nehemiah to put the walls together.

Nehemiah. He would not let these people stop Nehemiah. Nehemiah was doing something that God wanted.

At last the walls were put together. Many people came to see the new walls. They thanked God for these beautiful walls. And they thanked God for sending Nehemiah to help them.

Will you do one thing for God this week?

New Words I Have Learned

Nehemiah	outside	strong
tore	tried	wall
	soldier	

New Thoughts to Think About

1. What if Nehemiah had not gone to his home city? The walls may never have been put together again.
2. What if you do not obey God or your mother and father? Do you think that something may never get done?

New Things for Me to Do

Make some pictures of boys and girls who are helpers. What can you do to help God? Ask Mother or Father what you can do to help Him. Will you do one thing for God this week?

Being
Sorry

God's People Are Sorry

"I don't like our food," said a man.

"I don't like to live here," said a woman. "Why did Moses bring us here?"

"God does not help us," they said. "Moses does not help us, either. No one helps us."

There were snakes everywhere.

Moses was very sad when he heard what the people said. He did not like to hear the people say these things. God did not like it either.

God had done many things for His people. He had helped them go away from Egypt. They were not slaves now. They did not have to work for the king.

But the people were not happy. They wanted more food. They wanted better things. They wanted God to do more for them.

God was angry at His people. So He sent something to show them that He was angry. "Snakes!" the people said. "Run!"

But the people could not run away from the snakes. There were snakes everywhere.

"We will die," the people said.

Some of the people did die. The snakes made them die.

Now the other people were more afraid. "God sent these snakes," they said. "He is angry with us."

The people went to see Moses. "God is angry with us," they said. "He is hurting us with the snakes. He is hurting us because we have said bad things. Please help us."

Moses listened to God's people. He wanted to help them.

"Ask God to take the snakes away," the people said.

Moses talked with God. He asked God to take the snakes away.

But God did not take the snakes away. He told Moses how to help the people.

"Make a big brass snake," God said. "Put it on a pole. The people who look at it will not die."

Moses made the big brass snake. He put it on a pole. Then he told the people what God had said.

God told the people to look at the big brass snake.

When you do something bad, tell Jesus you are sorry.

"Look at the brass snake," Moses told the people. "Then you will not die when the snakes bite you."

"We are sorry for the things we said," the people told Moses. "We will look at the brass snake. We will not say bad things about God again."

New Words I Have Learned

either   brass   sin

snake   pole   sorry

       pray

New Thoughts to Think About

1. Was it right for the people to say bad things about God? Bad things that hurt God are called sin.

2. Have you done bad things that hurt God? Yes, we all have.

3. Jesus died to take away our sin. When we are sorry, we tell Him so. Moses' people obeyed God by looking at the snake. We obey God by telling Jesus we are sorry. When we talk to Jesus, we pray.

New Things for Me to Do

Write the words **sin, sorry,** and **pray** and put them in your room. Each time you do something bad, or sin, look at those words. They will tell you to be sorry and talk to Jesus.

One night, Nicodemus went to
talk with Jesus.

Jesus Tells How to Be Sorry

Nicodemus did not like what his friends said about Jesus. He did not like to hear them say that Jesus was a bad man.

"Jesus does many wonderful things," Nicodemus thought. "He does things that my friends can not do."

Nicodemus knew that Jesus was not like other people. Jesus had something that other people did not have.

One night Nicodemus went to see Jesus. He wanted to talk about these things.

"God sent You to the world," Nicodemus said. "I know this. No other person can do the wonderful things You do."

Then Jesus and Nicodemus began to talk about Heaven. They talked about the way to get to Heaven.

Nicodemus was glad that he had talked with Jesus.

"When you came into this world, you were born," said Jesus. "If you want to go into Heaven, you must be born once more."

"But how can I become a baby again?" Nicodemus asked.

Jesus looked at the trees. The wind was blowing in them.

"Do you know where the wind comes from?" Jesus asked. "Do you know where it goes?"

Nicodemus thought for a while. "No," he said. "I know it is there. But I do not know where it comes from. I do not know where it goes."

"When you are born once more, you know it has been done," said Jesus. "But you do not know how."

"How can these things be true?" Nicodemus asked.

"I know they are true," said Jesus. "I have lived with God in Heaven."

Nicodemus knew that Jesus was right. He knew that Jesus was God's Son. Jesus had seen many things that others had never seen.

"God loves the world very much," said Jesus.

"He sent His Son to the world to die for people. God wants you to be sorry for the bad things you do. He wants you to love Him. He wants you to live with Him when you die."

Nicodemus was glad that he had talked with Jesus. He wanted to be born once more so he could go to Heaven. Then he would always live with Jesus, God's Son.

Have you ever asked Jesus to help you get to Heaven? Would you like to do that now?

New Words I Have Learned

baby   wind   Heaven

become   blow   Nicodemus

                     born

New Thoughts to Think About

1. Jesus told Nicodemus how to get to Heaven. What did He say?

2. Why did Jesus know so much about Heaven? Had He lived there? Who was Jesus' Father?

New Things for Me to Do

Have you ever asked Jesus to help you get to Heaven? Would you like to do that now? Here is the way to do it.

1. Are you sorry that you have done bad things? Tell Jesus that you are sorry. Ask Jesus to keep these bad thir.gs from hurting you.

2. Ask Jesus to make you into a new boy or girl. He will. That is when you are "born again." You don't do some things you did before. You do things that God wants you to do.

The Boy Who Was Sorry

"I want to go away from home," a boy told his father.

The boy's father was very sad. He knew that the boy wanted to do things he could not do at home.

"Give me some money," the boy said. "I must have some money to live away from home."

The boy was not little. He was a young man. So the father did not make him stay at home.

The father gave the boy some money. But the boy did not say "thank you." He did not even say "good-bye."

The father watched the boy go away. "Will he come home again?" the father thought.

The boy did not care what his father thought. He did not care that his father was very sad. He thought only of the fun he would have away from home.

The father was very sad
when his boy went away.

"I will go far away," the boy said. "Then my father can not stop me from having fun."

The boy's fun was not good fun. He did only what he wanted to do. He found friends who were not good people.

The boy's friends liked to have fun with him. They liked to help the boy spend his money.

But one day the boy's money was gone. He had nothing left.

"My friends will help me," the boy said.

But the boy's friends would not help him. "We liked you when you had money to spend," they said. "But we do not like you now."

The boy became very hungry. Now he had to work to get money.

"You may take care of my pigs," a man said.

The boy did not like to take care of pigs. He thought about his home. He thought about

**The boy was sorry
that he had made his father sad.**

the people who worked for his father. They
had more than he had.

Then the boy thought about all the bad things
he had done. He was sorry now that he had
done them. He was sorry that he had made his
father sad.

"I will go home," he said one day. "I will

When you hurt someone, tell him that you are sorry.

tell my father that I am sorry for the bad things I have done."

The father was so happy to have his boy come home. He was happy to have his boy with him again.

"I thought my boy would never come back," the father said. "But now he has come home to stay."

New Words I Have Learned

young   fun   spend

good-bye   pigs

New Thoughts to Think About

1. Was this boy good or bad? Did his father love him, even when he was bad? But did his father love the bad things he did?

2. Does your Father in Heaven love you? Does He love you even when you are bad? But does He love the bad things you do?

3. How did this boy make things right again? He told his father he was sorry. How do you make things right again? You tell God you are sorry. When you hurt someone, you tell him that you are sorry.

New Things for Me to Do

Think of something you have done that may hurt Mother or Father. Tell them you are sorry.

What These Stories Teach

Each story in this book teaches an important Bible truth, or doctrine. Each story also teaches an important truth about the child's daily living.

These two truths, or objectives, often are so closely related within a story that they may not be obvious to the parent or teacher. All objectives, doctrinal and present-day, are listed here so they may be clearly understood by the parent or teacher.

Story	Doctrinal objectives	Present-day objectives
God Gives a Beautiful World	God is the Creator of all things.	We should thank God for His beautiful creation.
	God takes care of all His creation, including us.	We should thank God for taking care of His world and us.
God Takes Care of Joseph	God is able to help people in need.	We should ask God to help us when we need help.
Food for Hungry People	God is the Giver of all food and water.	When we need food, we should ask God for some.
		When we have food, we should thank God for giving it to us.
Some Good People Share Their House	God wants His people to share with each other.	We should share our homes and food with other Christians.
Wise Men Share Their Best	God gives His best gifts to us.	We should give our best gifts to God.
	He deserves our best gifts in return.	

A Boy Shares His Food	Jesus can multiply our gifts to Him.	We should help Jesus do His work by giving what we can to Him.
Abraham Obeys God	God wants His people to obey Him by doing what He says.	We should do anything God wants us to do.
Moses Obeys God	God wants His people to obey Him by going where He says.	We should go anywhere God wants us to go.
Nehemiah Does What God Wants	God wants His people to obey Him by working for Him.	We should do the work God wants us to do, even though others may try to stop us.
God's People Are Sorry	God wants to forgive our sin and has made a way for us to be forgiven, through His Son, Jesus.	We should tell God that we are sorry for our sin and ask Him to forgive us.
Jesus Tells How to Be Sorry	Jesus has made a way for us to get to Heaven.	We should ask Jesus to help us get to Heaven by taking away our sin and giving us a new life.
	Jesus knows about Heaven because He lived there before He was on earth.	
	Jesus wants to help people get to Heaven.	
The Boy Who Was Sorry	God loves us, even though we sin, and wants us to come back to Him and ask for forgiveness.	We should make things right with God by turning away from our sin and going to Him for forgiveness.

Basic Word List

Your child probably knows the 323 basic words listed below, or at least most of them. This list has been compiled primarily from standard word lists used in public school education, as well as from the most frequently used words in basic reading textbooks.

New words, words not included in this basic list, are given with each Bible story. A cumulative list of new words follows this one.

Variants of a word are not considered new words. These include words made by adding s, es, ies, ing, ed, er, est, iest, or ly. Thus, talks, talked, and talking are not considered new words since talk is on the basic word list.

a	away	but	does
about	back	by	done
afraid	bad	cake	don't
again	basket	call	down
ago	be	came	each
all	beautiful	can	eat
alone	became	care	enough
along	because	chair	even
also	bed	children	every
always	been	church	everyone
am	before	city	everything
and	began	climb	everywhere
angry	best	clothes	far
animal	better	cold	father
another	big	come	field
any	bird	could	find
anyone	bite	country	fire
anything	bow	cut	first
are	boy	day	fish
around	brave	did	five
as	bread	die	flower
ask	break	dig	follow
at	broke	dirt	food
ate	brought	do	found

for	if	men
friend	I'll	money
from	I'm	more
full	in	mother
gave	into	mountain
get	is	much
giant	it	must
gift	jar	my
girl	just	name
give	keep	near
glad	kill	need
go	kind	never
goes	king	new
good	kitchen	next
gone	knew	night
grass	know	no
ground	lake	not
grow	last	nothing
had	laugh	now
hand	lay	obey
happy	lead	of
have	learn	on
he	left	once
hear	let	one
heard	let's	only
help	letter	or
her	light	other
here	like	our
hide	little	out
him	live	over
his	long	paper
hole	look	people
home	love	pick
house	made	picture
how	make	place
hungry	man	please
hurry	many	pull
hurt	may	put
I	me	rain

ran	such	up
right	sudden	us
river	table	very
road	take	wait
rode	talk	walk
room	tell	want
rope	ten	was
run	than	watch
sad	thank	water
said	that	way
same	the	we
sat	their	week
saw	them	well
say	then	went
see	there	were
seen	these	what
sell	they	when
send	thing	where
sent	think	while
she	this	who
sheep	thought	why
should	those	wide
shout	three	will
show	time	wish
sing	tire	with
sky	to	woman
sleep	together	won
smile	told	wonderful
so	too	word
sold	took	work
some	town	world
someone	tree	would
something	true	write
soon	two	year
stand	under	yes
stay	until	you
stop		your

New Word List

The following is a cumulative list of the seventy-one new words used in this volume. These words are listed with each Bible story where they first appear.

These are words which appear in the Bible stories, but do not appear in the basic word list.

No more than seven new words are used with each Bible story. Often a smaller number is used to give the child a change of pace. This permits him to read for enjoyment as well as for learning.

Many of the new words are "specialized vocabulary words" because the stories are Bible-related. The specialized Bible words will help to acquaint your beginning reader with Bible names and terms which he should begin to know.

Abraham	coat	lamp	snake
Adam	dream	listen	soldier
altar	drink	loaves	Son
angel	Egypt	manna	sorry
baby	either	Mary	spend
become	Elisha	moon	star
Bethlehem	Eve	Moses	strong
Bible	evening	Nehemiah	stone
blow	fun	Nicodemus	sun
born	God	outside	taste
brass	good-bye	piece	tore
brother	Heaven	pigs	tried
burn	Herod	pole	wall
bush	husband	pray	wife
camel	Isaac	princess	wind
careful	jail	share	wise
caught	Jesus	sin	young
cent	Joseph	slave